NELSON MANDELA

REGGIE FINLAYSON

In Consultation with Martha Cosgrove,
M.A. and Reading Specialist

JUST THE FACTS BIOGRAPHIES

◿ LERNER PUBLICATIONS COMPANY / MINNEAPOLIS

Martha Cosgrove has a master's degree from the University of Minnesota in secondary education, with an emphasis on developmental and remedial reading. She is licensed in 7–12 English and language arts, developmental reading, and remedial reading. She has had several works published, and she gives numerous state and national presentations in her areas of expertise.

Lerner Publications Company
A division of Lerner Publishing Group
241 First Avenue North
Minneapolis, Minnesota 55401 U.S.A.

Website address: www.lernerbooks.com

Library of Congress Cataloging-in-Publication Data

Finlayson, Reggie.
    Nelson Mandela / by Reggie Finlayson.
        p.   cm. – (Just the facts biographies)
    Includes bibliographical references and index.
    ISBN-13: 978-0-8225-2644-5 (lib. bdg. : alk. paper)
    ISBN-10: 0-8225-2644-1 (lib. bdg. : alk. paper)
    1. Mandela, Nelson, 1918– –Juvenile literature. 2. Presidents–South Africa–Biography–Juvenile literature. I. Title. II. Series.
    DT1974.F56 2006
    968.06'5'092–dc22   2005013166

Manufactured in the United States of America
1 2 3 4 5 6 – BP – 11 10 09 08 07 06

CONTENTS

1

BIRTH OF A LEADER

THE MORNING OF MAY 10, 1994,

was bright and clear. Leaders from around the world had gathered in Pretoria, South Africa. Everyone was excited. Visitors from Europe, Asia, Africa, and the United States took their places in the meeting room. Blacks and whites sat side by side. An African man was being sworn in as president.

Ten years earlier, this meeting would not have happened. Back then, South Africa was locked in a huge and violent battle for equality between the races. But that time was a memory

**(Above)
Nelson
Mandela
made history
in 1994
when he was
sworn in as
Sout Africa's
first black
president.**

that many hoped would quickly fade. The world's leaders were in Pretoria to mark the change. South Africa was becoming a brand new nation. In this nation, all races would be treated equally by the law.

Nelson Rolihlahla Mandela had just been elected the first black president of South Africa. He walked across the stage like a lion. Everyone looked at him. He was seventy-six years old. He had spent nearly thirty years in South African prisons. Yet he walked like a young man. He had become a symbol of survival and freedom. He greeted the kings, queens, presidents, and prime ministers in the audience. They leaned forward in their seats so they wouldn't miss a word he said.

Mandela said that their meeting gave "hope to newborn liberty." Many people had fought to change South Africa. Like him, many had been in prisons. Many had died. Mandela's voice was powerful. He spoke for all of those people.

Mandela had known too much violence and hatred in his life. He spoke about the chance for peace and dignity. The new South Africa would put "hope in the breasts of the millions of our people," he said. He talked about building a South Africa where white people and black people would both feel pride.

Both could walk down streets without fear. South Africa would become "a rainbow nation at peace with itself and the world."

The audience nodded and clapped. Mandela's own example offered hope to South Africans. It also gave hope to the rest of the world. He had stood up for the rights of all people in South Africa. And he had spent time in prison for opposing the South African government. Yet he could not be held down. He was ready to continue the fight. At his age, most people retire. But Nelson Mandela was taking control of a new nation in which all people would be equal.

EARLY DAYS

Rolihlahla Mandela was born on July 18, 1918, in the small village of Mvezo in South Africa. Mvezo sits in the Transkei region—an area of rolling hills, valleys, and streams. It is about 800 miles east of Cape Town (South Africa's largest city) and 550 miles south of the city of Johannesburg. It lies next to the blue waters of the Indian Ocean.

The Transkei region is the traditional homeland of the Xhosa. The Xhosa are one of the largest ethnic groups in South Africa.

WHO IS WHO, WHAT IS WHAT

African National Congress (ANC): founded in 1912, the organization that pushed for civil rights in South Africa

apartheid [ah-PAHR-tayt]: a set of laws that restricted the rights of nonwhite South Africans

Johannesburg: a large South African city where Nelson Mandela began living and working in the early 1940s

Jongintaba [jun-geen-TAH-bah]: the acting king of the Thembu clan who became Mandela's guardian in 1927

Mphakanyiswa [m-pah-gah-NEEZ-wah]: Mandela's father, who died when Nelson was nine

Nationalist Party: the political group that made apartheid (apartness) the law in South Africa

Oliver Tambo: a schoolmate of Mandela's with whom he'd later open a law practice. Tambo and Mandela also started the ANC Youth League together.

Robben Island: the location of the prison where Mandela spent nearly twenty-seven years

Rolihlahla [ho-lee-SHAH-shah]: Mandela's boyhood name

Thembu [TEM-boo]: the clan of the Xhosa nation to which Mandela belongs

Transkei [trahn-SKY]: the area of southeastern South Africa where Mandela grew up

Walter Sisulu: an ANC member whom Mandela met when he first went to Johannesburg. Together, Sisulu and Mandela would serve prison terms at Robben Island.

Winnie Mandela: Mandela's second wife

Xhosa [KOH-sah]: the African nation to which Mandela belongs

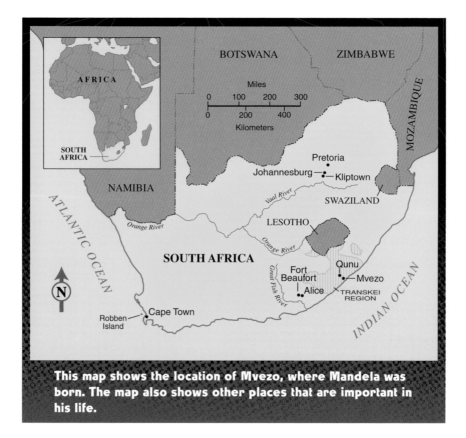

This map shows the location of Mvezo, where Mandela was born. The map also shows other places that are important in his life.

Rolihlahla was born into the Thembu clan, part of the Xhosa nation. From the beginning, he was taught the culture of this group. At birth, he was not called Nelson. Instead, he had the traditional Xhosa name Rolihlahla. Xhosa people were given names that described them in some way or suggested what they might become. Rolihlahla means "pulling the branch of a tree." Gadla Henry Mphakanyiswa, Rolihlahla's father, gave this name to his son.

Rolihlahla was born into a royal family. His father was a minor chief in the village of Mvezo. He was like a mayor. He kept business moving in the village. He also settled disputes. Sometimes he acted as a judge and decided cases according to tribal law. He also served as a sort of prime minister, or chief adviser, to the highest tribal authority, the Thembu king.

Rolihlahla loved his father. He was very proud of his father's experience and wisdom. He was also proud of the way people in the community looked up to him. His father gave Rolihlahla his first lessons in being a leader.

During the 1920s, the Xhosa king died suddenly. But the boy who was in line to be the next king was too young. People argued over who should be king while they waited for the boy to grow up.

IT'S A FACT!

As a boy, Mandela would rub white ashes into the hair above his forehead. He wanted to look more like his father, who had white hair in that same spot.

Rolihlahla's father favored a man who was fairly low in rank. But the man was the best educated. His name was Jongintaba.

Mphakanyiswa's opinion carried the day. Jongintaba became acting king, or regent. The elders soon saw that it was the best decision. Jongintaba would bring wisdom and good fortune to the Xhosa people.

A LEGACY OF STRUGGLE

During Rolihlahla's youth, society was changing quickly. Many people had new ideas about religion, housing, clothing, and marriage. Many neighbors threw out the old ideas. But Rolihlahla's father held onto the traditional way of life.

According to custom, Mphakanyiswa had four wives. Among the four wives, Mphakanyiswa had thirteen children. He had four boys and nine girls. Rolihlahla's mother was the third wife. Rolihlahla was the oldest of his mother's children. But he was the youngest male among all his father's children.

The entire family did not live together under one roof. Each wife had her own kraal. A kraal is a living area in the countryside. It included one or more huts to live in. It also had fields for farming and a pen for

A Xhosa chief, Moqoma *(center)*, in the 1800s, with his four wives

animals. The kraals of the four wives were similar. But they were separated by several miles. Rolihlahla's father divided his time equally among them.

Mphakanyiswa was a proud man. He was wealthy by Xhosa standards. People in his community respected him. But even a wealthy and respected Xhosa man did not have much status in South African society.

By this time, South Africa had become a nation made up of many races of people. The vast majority of the people are black and belong to different ethnic groups. These groups include the Xhosa, the Zulu, the Ndebele, and the Swazi. The country's whites are also from different backgrounds.

Most of South Africa's whites are Afrikaners. This group's ancestors came to South Africa from the Netherlands in the mid-1600s. The other group of whites—sometimes called Anglo-African—has British ancestors. South Africa also has a small population of East Indians.

European nations had fought for control over parts of Africa for hundreds of years. In South Africa, the Dutch eventually lost out to the British in 1902. The British still controlled South Africa during Rolihlahla's childhood. At that time, local chiefs reported not only to their tribal kings. They also reported to white magistrates, officials appointed by the British.

AFRIKANERS

The first Dutch settlers came to South Africa in 1652. They were looking for new trade routes. Soon afterward, they set up the Cape Colony and began moving into lands already lived in by African ethnic groups. Over time, the Dutch settlers came to call themselves Afrikaners. In 1820, British settlers arrived in the Cape Colony. At the time, Britain was the world's most powerful country. The British-descended white settlers competed for land and power with the Afrikaners. This competition eventually led to war in 1899. By 1902, the Afrikaners had agreed to a peace treaty that put the country under British control.

These magistrates had more power and status than the tribal authorities. They had the final say in making decisions.

Soon after Rolihlahla was born, his father made a mistake. He acted as if he were equal to a white magistrate. The magistrate charged Mphakanyiswa with not following orders and removed him from office. White officials in South Africa got a second chance if they made a mistake. But Mphakanyiswa, a black man, did not. The magistrate stripped Rolihlahla's father of his position and the money that came with the position. But the magistrate could not take Mphakanyiswa's dignity. He could not take his pride and respect.

VILLAGE LIFE

Mphakanyiswa was no longer chief. With less money in the family, Rolihlahla's mother decided to move. She and her children moved a few miles away to a smaller village called Qunu. It was closer to her family. The new village had just a few hundred people. Rolihlahla's mother had three huts: one for cooking, one for sleeping, and one for storage.

Mandela grew up in the Transkei region of South Africa in a Xhosa village like this one.

The huts were round and had mud walls. Their angled, grass roofs were supported by wooden poles. The doorways were so low that people had to stoop to enter. The huts were set away from fields of corn, sorghum, beans, and pumpkins. Rolihlahla's family ate what they grew.

Like most blacks, Rolihlahla's family was not allowed to own their own land, however. Instead, the government owned the land. Still, Rolihlahla's childhood was happy. He was a herd boy who tended sheep and cattle. Like all Xhosa, he learned to love cattle. To the Xhosa, cattle represented food, wealth, a source of happiness, and a blessing from God.

Qunu was a tightly knit community. People related to one another more as family than as neighbors. Whites didn't enter this world very often. But the local government official was white. So was the owner of the nearest store. Sometimes white travelers and white police officers passed through the small village. But they were rare visitors.

LEARNING NEW LESSONS

Most of the villagers in Qunu were Xhosa. But there were also some Mfengu villagers. These people had come into Xhosa territory about one hundred years earlier. The Mfengu lived as a people apart in the land of the Xhosa. The Xhosa looked down on the Mfengu and forced them to do the jobs nobody else wanted.

Rolihlahla's father was different from most of the Xhosa. He judged people on their actions instead of on their ethnic origins. He urged his son to do the same. Rolihlahla watched his father make friends with many people, no matter what their ethnicity or religion was. One such friendship was with a Mfengu man. It would have a great effect on Rolihlahla's early life.

Ben Mbekela was a retired Mfengu teacher. He noticed Rolihlahla's curiosity and intelligence. He told Rolihlahla's parents that their son might have a bright future if he were educated in one of the new schools near the village. No one in the family had ever attended school. But Rolihlahla's father liked the idea right away. At the age of seven, Rolihlahla enrolled in the local Methodist school.

Rolihlahla even got a new name. His teacher politely told him that his new name was Nelson. Nobody knows why the teacher chose Nelson. Nelson first thought he was renamed because Europeans had trouble pronouncing African names. But later he wondered if his teacher had been trying to separate him from his Xhosa culture.

DEATH IN THE FAMILY

When Nelson was nine, his father arrived at his mother's home. Mphakanyiswa usually divided his time evenly among the homes of his four wives. The schedule was always the same. So Nelson and

his mother were surprised when Mphakanyiswa
showed up several days early. They were also
surprised by how sick he looked. He had lost
weight and coughed violently, almost without
stopping. He complained about his lungs. Like
many Xhosa people, Mphakanyiswa had a great
passion for smoking. His health problems were
likely a result of this habit.

Nelson's mother did what she could to care for
Mphakanyiswa. But nothing could relieve the
hacking cough. Then Mphakanyiswa called for his
wife to bring his tobacco and pipe. She was afraid
that smoking would only make things worse.
Rolihlahla's father insisted, and she finally gave in.
Mphakanyiswa took a deep draw on the pipe. He
stopped coughing and was suddenly calm. For
another hour or so, he continued to smoke. Then
he quietly died. The pipe was still lit.

The elders claimed it was a blessing for a man
to die so peacefully. But Nelson was very sad. His
father had given him his sense of who he was. With
his father gone, Nelson's life changed greatly.

CHAPTER 2

IN THE ROYAL KRAAL

SHORTLY AFTER Mphakanyiswa's funeral, Nelson's mother told him that he, as her only son, was to leave Qunu. The news was a shock. But Nelson didn't question her about where he was going or why. African children did not question their elders. Nelson simply packed and got ready to go.

He and his mother started out early in the day. The morning sun was warm. They climbed a hill near Qunu. Nelson looked down at the houses, fields, and forest. He wondered if he would ever see his home again. He tried hard to burn the scene into his memory. He

Like these young men, Mandela became skilled at stick fighting.

thought about his friends herding cattle, stick fighting, and playing in the forest. He already missed them.

A NEW LIFE

Nelson and his mother walked all day. They barely talked. Then, late in the afternoon, they entered a village. In the center was a set of buildings. They reminded Nelson of the huts in his mother's village. But the fine roofs seemed incredibly high. The walls were whitewashed and shining in the sun.

Nelson had never seen buildings so beautiful. Nearby were neatly tended gardens, fertile fields, fruit trees, and herds of cattle and sheep.

Some fancy cars pulled into the village. Several men stepped from the cars. One of them came toward the two travelers with his hand out. He was Jongintaba–regent of the Thembu clan of the Xhosa nation.

Jongintaba! His name means "one who looks at the mountain." This was the man Nelson's father had supported to be acting king of the Xhosa so

Chief Jongintaba (right) became Mandela's guardian after Mphakanyiswa's death.

many years before. Jongintaba had sent for Nelson.
From now on, the regent would watch over Nelson
as his guardian. Nelson and his mother were
warmly received. The people of the village treated
them well. This was to be Nelson's new home.

Nelson missed his mother when she left, but
he soon got used to his
new life. Jongintaba and
his wife treated Nelson
like their own son. Nelson
was like a brother to the
regent's two children,
especially to the regent's
son, Justice. Nelson ate
with the family and slept
in their house.

Nelson's new home
was the center of tribal
government for the
Thembu. The regent

IT'S A FACT!

Mandela had a lot of
respect for Justice,
Jongintaba's son.
Mandela tried to be
like him in many
ways. But the two
boys were very
different. Mandela
was quite serious,
and Justice was
quite carefree.

called meetings to talk about such issues as drought,
caring for cattle, and new laws and rules. All tribal
members were welcome, and every man was given
the chance to speak. The men talked and argued
until everyone agreed.

Nelson lived in this hut under Jongintaba's care.

In later years, Nelson would remember what took place in the royal kraal. It would affect his own leadership style. The system had flaws, but it also had value. Watching the process made Nelson even more interested in history and the ways in which people might work together.

Visiting chiefs fascinated Nelson. Many were wise and spoke well. Nelson was particularly impressed by an old chief who loved to tell stories about the Xhosa heroes of the past. Nelson loved to sit and listen to these tales.

STEPPING-STONES TO MANHOOD

Nelson was being trained, although he didn't know it. He was being prepared to hold a position his father had held—adviser to the king. By the time he was sixteen, Nelson had become an impressive young man. But he was not yet an adult. The rite of circumcision would make him an adult in the eyes of the tribal community.

Circumcision is an operation. It removes the foreskin of a young man's penis. It is a minor operation that takes several minutes. But the actual procedure was not as important as what it meant. It meant a transferring of Xhosa values and a sense of group unity. Before the operation and during the recovery, boys were taught what it meant to be a Xhosa adult.

BEFORE AND AFTER CIRCUMCISION

Before the circumcision ritual, the young men had to perform a daring task. Mandela and his friends decided their task would be to steal a pig from another person in the tribe. Mandela claims that no pork has ever tasted better. After the ceremony, Mandela received two cows and four sheep. Justice received an entire herd. For the Xhosa, livestock are forms of wealth. Mandela was filled with pride and excitement over his newly found wealth.

After the circumcision, Nelson and other young men his age rested. They stayed in huts until they were healed. Afterward, the huts were burned to the ground with all the contents inside. The boys' last links to childhood were destroyed. They were then considered men. Villagers watched as the young men were presented to the tribe in a ceremony. Proud parents showered their children with gifts. Nelson was proud to take his place in the adult world of his people.

Many people spoke that day. One was a man named Chief Meligqili. He stood and looked at the crowd. Then he looked at the young men and started to speak:

> There sit our sons: young, healthy, and handsome, the flower of the Xhosa tribe, the pride of our nation. We have just circumcised them in a ritual that promises them manhood, but I am here to tell you that it is an empty, illusory promise, a promise than can never be fulfilled. For we Xhosas, and all black South Africans are a conquered people.

Suddenly, the mood shifted. Smiles fell away from the faces of parents and children alike. They clearly did not want to hear this kind of talk. But the old man pressed on. He said that blacks in South Africa were slaves in their own country. The young men at the ceremony that day would go to cities where they would end up living in shacks. They would work in mines for white people. They would never own land or become successful, because white people owned everything.

The words washed over Nelson, and he became very angry at the speaker. This was to have been one of the happiest days of his life. This man had ruined it with his talk. Nelson wished those words had never been spoken. He tried to flush them from his mind. But the words had seeped into his soul. He knew that his childhood had ended that day, along with childish ideas about the world.

3 GOING TO SCHOOL

IN 1934, at the age of sixteen, Nelson continued going to school. Most African children received only a few years of schooling before taking jobs. But Mandela was not meant to work in South Africa's mines or in a white farmer's field. He was to be the adviser to kings.

He went to Clarkebury Boarding Institute. It was one of the best schools for black youths in southern Africa. Children from many of the area's best families went there. Living with Jongintaba, Nelson was used to getting respect. But he quickly found that he no longer stood out. Nearly everyone in his school was just as important in their home villages. Then he went on to a school named Healdtown, located in Fort Beaufort.

AT HEALDTOWN

Healdtown was more tolerant of African cultures than some other European institutions. But the instructors still believed that Africans were backward. This attitude rubbed off on the students. They believed they were backward and inferior.

Even so, Healdtown did produce disciplined scholars. Students were up at 6:00 A.M. and continued their academic day until 5:00 P.M. Then they had dinner, an hour break, and two hours of study hall. They had to be in their rooms by 9:30 P.M. This schedule developed the mental muscles of the students.

In Nelson's final year at Healdtown, Samuel Krune Mqhayi visited the school. Mqhayi was a poet who had written part of the South African national anthem. Mqhayi spoke at Nelson's school. "We cannot allow these foreigners who do not care for our culture to take over our nation," Mqhayi warned. "I predict that one day, the forces of African society will achieve a [huge] victory."

By the end of high school, Mandela already showed signs of leadership.

The words awakened something in Nelson. They made him think of the regent's royal kraal and the heroes in the old chief's tales. He remembered the disturbing words Chief Meligqili had spoken at the circumcision rites.

The chief had described the Xhosa as being under white control.

Mqhayi's words were magical. When the poet moved, all eyes followed. The students' spirits rose and fell as Mqhayi's voice rose and fell. When the poet finished speaking, the students stood with thunderous applause. Nelson felt himself touched in a deep way. Like many students, he had come to doubt the ability of Africans to compete with Europeans. But Mqhayi made Nelson remember the great power of his own roots. He had never felt any prouder to be Xhosa than at that moment.

HIGHER LEARNING

In 1940, World War II (1939–1945) was raging in Europe. Nelson Mandela was twenty-one years old. That year, he began his first year at the all-black University College of Fort Hare. The college is located in the town of Alice, South Africa. The school was a small college. There were only 150 students, and they were among the brightest in southern Africa.

Nelson had long dreamed of this day. He believed education was the key to success in the

University College of Fort Hare in the early 1940s

modern world. Fort Hare was the finest school
available to a Xhosa man. Since a number of other
students had been his schoolmates before, he felt at
home there. Many students were new to him, but
they seemed to be much like him. Among them
was Oliver Tambo. Oliver would become a lifelong
friend and political partner of Nelson's.

From the start, Nelson planned to study law.
This would help him in his role as tribal adviser. In

his first year, his studies included Roman Dutch law and Native Administration—a class about laws affecting Africans. Many of these laws were intended to keep blacks and whites apart.

At the time, Nelson believed race relations were getting better in his country. But then Nelson met fellow students Nyathi Khongisa and Paul Mahabane. The two were known as rebels. They introduced Nelson to the African National Congress (ANC).

OLIVER TAMBO, MANDELA'S FELLOW STUDENT

Oliver Reginald Tambo was born on October 27, 1917. His parents named him Kaizana, after the German leader and enemy of Britain, Kaiser Wilhelm II.

When Kaizana entered school, he changed his name to Oliver. He soon found that he didn't enjoy school. His teachers were strict, and the lessons were dull. Things didn't change until he met another boy who was a great debater. Oliver then realized that he, too, could learn things in school that would help him be a great debater. Oliver attended Holy Cross, a missionary school in another town, and then attended Saint Peters in Johannesburg. From there, he enrolled at University College where he met Nelson Mandela for the first time. Like Mandela, Tambo was expelled for participating in the student strike. He returned to Saint Peters and worked there as a math and science teacher. During that time, he became involved in the African National Congress.

Nelson learned that the ANC had been started in 1912 to work for racial equality in South Africa. Its members were mostly middle-class urban blacks and royal members of tribes. The ANC wanted to work for change in South Africa through peaceful protest and by teaching people about racial injustice in South Africa.

Learning about the ANC changed the way Nelson thought about himself. He stopped looking

In 1914, several ANC leaders visited Britain. They were there to discuss racial injustice in South Africa.

at himself as simply a Xhosa man. He began to see himself as an African. The ANC helped turn him into an activist. He was ready to work actively to fight injustice.

His new attitude got him into trouble with the school. Fort Hare students wanted a stronger voice in the running of their school. To protest for more student rights, Nelson and others convinced students not to take part in student government elections. As a result, Nelson was kicked out of the school.

COUNTRY BOY, CITY MAN

Nelson was troubled on his ride back to the royal kraal. He knew that Jongintaba, the Thembu regent, would be unhappy that he had been kicked out of school. Jongintaba expected Nelson to complete his degree and to become an adviser to the tribal king. Nelson did not look forward to explaining what had happened.

During their first meeting, Jongintaba did not shout. He didn't have to. He simply ordered Nelson to find a way to pick up his education again. There was no sense in arguing, so Nelson agreed. He left the matter alone for the time being.

Things returned to normal for Nelson at the royal kraal. He ran errands for Jongintaba and looked after some of his affairs. It was life as he had known it since he had left his mother's home at the age of nine. The dress, conversations, and schedules were the same. Yet Nelson saw the world much differently. He realized that he had changed. He was no longer the country boy who had left for school years before.

Shortly after Nelson's return, Jongintaba announced that he needed to put his affairs in order. Jongintaba was getting old. At the top of his list was the well-being of his son, Justice, and of Nelson. As part of his plan, Jongintaba had even chosen a wife for Nelson. He had already set up the wedding.

Nelson was horrified. He knew the young woman who had been chosen. She was nice, but Nelson did not love her. Besides, he was not ready to settle down. There was too much of the world left to explore.

Nelson was torn. He had been raised to respect his elders. But he was not willing to accept an arranged marriage. He considered himself a modern African man. An arranged marriage was

NO WIVES FOR US!

The wife chosen for Mandela wasn't interested in marrying him. She actually liked Justice, the regent's son. Both Justice and Mandela fled from their arranged marriages. Jongintaba thought they might run away and told the local train station not to sell tickets to the young men. The two went to the next station to get tickets. But they still didn't have the right travel documents. The young men wound up getting a ride from a white woman. She charged them more than the cost of train tickets to Johannesburg.

not a modern idea. He decided the only thing to do was to run.

Nelson did not only run away from something he disliked. He also ran toward his destiny—to a place called Johannesburg.

CHAPTER
4
JOHANNESBURG

Mandela
moved to
Johannesburg
in the 1940s
(above). The
city was
already
divided into
white and
black areas.

IN THE EARLY 1940s, a wave of
people moved into Johannesburg and other
South African cities. Black villages offered few
jobs. So young blacks, especially men, headed
to the cities and surrounding mines looking
for work. Nelson Mandela was one of them.

Johannesburg is big and crowded. It
is South Africa's second-largest city. Rich
white suburbs are scattered throughout the
city. They were a world apart from the

shantytowns, or slums, where black people were forced to live at that time. The shantytowns were overcrowded and dirty. They had no electricity, no paved roads, and no telephones. Violence and family breakdowns were common. So were police raids. Seeing these towns gave Mandela an education he had not found at school.

Mandela needed a job, and his best chance seemed to be in the mines. South Africa has huge deposits of coal, gold, and diamonds. The mines employed many blacks. Mandela took a job as a security guard at a large gold mine. It was a good job compared with the dangers miners faced underground. In the mines, miners always had to worry about cave-ins. They also faced health risks from breathing dust.

Mandela moved into a large shantytown called Alexandria. Although the shantytown was poor, the place had energy.

IT'S A FACT!

Because of their connection with Jongintaba, Justice and Mandela were given important jobs at the mine in Johannesburg. Mandela became a security guard. Justice worked as a clerk in the office.

Mandela lived in a Johannesburg shantytown like this one.

Mandela would remember that energy fondly for years to come. He was amazed by his people's ability to find happiness and dignity in such conditions.

NEW TEACHERS

Alexandria attracted many black people. Some were criminals. Most were poor people just trying to survive. A few were leaders who cared about their people. Among this last group was Walter Sisulu.

WALTER SISULU

Born in 1912 to a Xhosa mother and a white father, Walter Sisulu grew up in the Transkei region. His mother's brother helped him understand the culture and values of the Xhosa. Sisulu received only a little schooling before going to Johannesburg to find work. He worked in the mines, in factories, and in bakeries. During his bakery job, he tried to organize his fellow workers to strike (stop working) for higher pay.

By 1940, Sisulu had joined the ANC. Throughout the 1950s, Sisulu actively supported black rule in South Africa. These activities eventually got him arrested several times. From 1963 to 1989, he was in prison with Mandela and other ANC leaders on Robben Island.

Walter Sisulu in the 1950s

Like Mandela, Sisulu came from the Transkei region. He was several years older than Mandela and had also worked in the mines. He was one of the lucky few who had moved on to a better job. He had become a real estate agent. He handled the few bits of land still available to blacks in Johannesburg.

Mandela impressed Sisulu from the start. The older man offered Mandela a job with a small salary. Mandela shared his plans with Sisulu. He wanted to complete his university bachelor's degree and to become a lawyer. Sisulu helped Mandela finish his degree through correspondence courses (taking classes through the mail).

Sisulu also introduced Mandela to the law firm of Witkin, Sidelsky and Eidelman. It was one of the largest firms in Johannesburg. It handled many real estate deals involving blacks. The firm hired Nelson to be a clerk while he was going to school. Many other firms would not hire any blacks.

On his first day at work for the law firm, he met Lazar Sidelsky, a partner in the firm. He seemed truly concerned with the suffering of black Africans. Sidelsky thought education was the key to progress for blacks in South Africa. He felt that an educated man like Mandela could do much to uplift the whole race. At the very least, successful black people would provide role models for others.

At first, Mandela agreed with Sidelsky's point of view. But then he got to know Gaur

Radebe, the other black clerk in the firm. Radebe changed Nelson's mind. "You people stole our land from us and enslaved us," Radebe once said to some white staff members. "Now you make us pay through the nose to get the worst pieces of it back."

Mandela discovered just how true those words were. Law firms did little actual work on the real estate sales. But they got most of the profits. The black agents received very little money for their work. Mandela's firm worked with Sisulu's real estate company. The firm always took most of the money from selling properties.

Mandela received his bachelor's degree from the University of South Africa in 1942. Soon after, he started law school at the University of Witwatersrand. He still worked for the law firm as a clerk. Meanwhile, Gaur Radebe and Walter Sisulu continued to teach him about racial equality.

JOINING THE ANC

Through his friendship with Walter Sisulu, Mandela finally joined the African National Congress (ANC). But Mandela did not simply become a member. He became a force within the organization.

**Mandela at an ANC
Youth League
Meeting.**

In 1944, Mandela, Walter Sisulu, Oliver
Tambo, and others formed the Youth League of the
ANC. Their goal was to bring real democracy to
South Africa. They would work for South Africans
of all races to be represented in government. (At
this time, only whites could vote and serve in
government in South Africa.) They would work for
the fair distribution of land and good education for
all. They wanted to end South Africa's unfair laws.

During the league's early stages, members
spent a lot of time planning. They worked out the
details of their organization. They met in the home
of Walter Sisulu. He and his wife, Albertina, were
like the parents many of the young men had left

behind. They offered plenty of food at their house. They always had a bed for people who needed a place to stay.

Mandela spent a lot of time at the Sisulu home. But politics wasn't the only pastime at the house. For Mandela, love grew there too. In 1944, he met a young woman from rural Transkei. Evelyn Mase was shy and pretty. She was training to be a nurse. She lived in nearby Orlando with her brother. She seemed a bit overwhelmed by the fast pace of life in the Sisulu household.

Nelson was touched by Evelyn's quiet beauty. He began dating her. Their romance moved quickly. Within a year, they were married in the city. It was a far different ceremony than Nelson would have had in the royal kraal. But he did not regret the choices he had made. He was happy with his life despite the hardships.

As a black couple, Nelson and Evelyn had

IT'S A FACT!

Mandela saw Jongintaba one time after running away to Johannesburg. Mandela was pleased that the meeting was friendly. Jongintaba didn't mention Mandela's disobedience.

Mandela and Evelyn Mase married in 1944.

trouble finding a decent house in Johannesburg. Blacks were allowed to live only in certain areas of the city. Finally, the couple found a small home in West Orlando, part of the township of Soweto. Townships were segregated (separate) areas where blacks and other non-Europeans were forced to live in South Africa. Soweto is just outside of Johannesburg. There, Nelson and Evelyn started a family. Their first child was born in 1946. They named their baby boy Madiba Thembelike Mandela. Within ten years, the couple would have

two more children. They had another son named
Makgatho. They also had a daughter who died
when she was just nine months old. All the while,
Mandela grew more involved with his work for
the African National Congress.

CHAPTER 5
A REVOLUTIONARY SPIRIT

WORLD WAR II in Europe ended in 1945. Germany's Nazi army was destroyed. Black South Africans had fought in the war against them. They were proud to have helped end the racism of the Nazi government. Next, they wanted to see racism end in their own country. ANC leaders, particularly in the Youth League, were hopeful.

By this time, South Africa was an independent nation. It had a peaceful relationship with Britain, its former ruler. Yet whites still governed South Africa with unfair, racist rule. In 1946, Prime Minister Jan Smut passed the Asiatic Land Tenure Act. This law was nicknamed the Ghetto Act. It forced East Indian people in South Africa to live only in certain ghettos, or poor neighborhoods. The law was a sharp reminder that discrimination was still alive in South Africa. All people of color—not just blacks—faced discrimination.

The East Indian community responded with a wave of protests. The protests continued for two years. Many of the East Indian leaders landed in jail. The ANC was greatly impressed by this effort.

In 1946, the National Indian Congress led a meeting. It protested the laws that kept East Indians from buying land in South Africa.

SOUTH AFRICA'S POPULATION MIX

About 80 percent of the people in South Africa are nonwhite. They are black, East Indian, or of mixed race. The South African government once named South Africans of mixed race "coloureds." Most of the country's whites are Afrikaners. They are descendants of Dutch settlers. The other whites are of British background. Sometimes they are called Anglo-Africans to separate them from the Afrikaners.

They were inspired by the East Indian leaders. The ANC no longer feared going to prison in the struggle for black civil rights.

A mine workers' strike in 1946 also made the ANC bolder. Mining for gold and diamonds is one of South Africa's largest industries. It produces much of the nation's wealth. But mining was dangerous, health-threatening work. Black miners were paid far less than white miners. Black workers had wanted change for years.

In 1946, about seventy thousand miners went on strike. They called for better pay and for a two-week paid vacation each year. They also demanded decent housing for workers and their families. The strike was led by J. B. Marks, president of the mine workers' union; Gaur Radebe; and Moses Kotane.

All were members of the ANC and of the Communist Party. (At this time, Communism—a system that gives most control to the government—was illegal in South Africa. The Communist Party was also illegal.)

Although the strike was nonviolent, it was illegal. The government sent a small army of police with rifles, bayonets, and batons against the strikers. Within a week, at least 9 miners had been killed and 1,248 others had been injured. The police brutally crushed the strike. Marks, Kotane, and 52 others were jailed.

THE NATIONALISTS

Things went from bad to worse for black South Africans. At this time, only whites could vote in South African elections. In 1948, the country's white voters elected Nationalist Party candidates into office. The Nationalists were led by Prime Minister Daniel Malan.

Malan and many other Nationalists were Afrikaners who disliked the British. Some Nationalists had even supported Germany—rather than Britain—during World War II. The Nationalists especially hated blacks. They warned voters about what they called the "black threat." During the campaign, the Nationalists often shouted insulting terms against blacks and East Indians.

Nationalist Party ideas could be grouped under one word, *apartheid*. It was a word few in the outside world had heard before. Apartheid means "apartness"–separation of the races. Some people in South Africa believed apartheid would help preserve the country's many cultures. But most South Africans saw apartheid for what it was. It was a new word for the old idea of white supremacy (rule).

In 1950, Malan's government passed two laws based on race. The first was the Population

Daniel Malan of the Nationalist Party was prime minister of South Africa from 1948 to 1954.

Registration Act. This law labeled everyone in South Africa according to race. The second was the Group Areas Act. It forced different racial groups to live in different places. These two laws were at the heart of apartheid.

In 1951, the government passed two more laws. One was the Separate Representation of Voters Act. Under this system, mixed race, or coloured, South Africans could vote. But their votes did not carry much weight. People they elected had no direct voice in government. That same year, the government ended the Native Representation Council. This was a group of black government advisers.

Attitudes toward blacks, coloureds, and East Indians hardened during this period. Apartheid controlled every area of work, schooling, housing, and family life by race. Nelson Mandela would later describe the system:

> An African child is born in an Africans Only hospital, taken home in an Africans Only bus, lives in an Africans Only area, and attends Africans Only schools, if he attends school at all. When he grows up, he can

hold Africans Only jobs, rent a house in
Africans Only townships, ride Africans Only
trains. . . .

By 1952, South Africa was almost totally
segregated. Afrikaners dominated all other ethnic
groups. It had been three hundred years since the
Afrikaners had set up a colony (settlement) in the
region. The Afrikaners saw their long survival as a
sign that they were God's chosen people. They set
out to outlaw nearly every form of protest.

LET AFRICA RETURN

By 1952, Nelson Mandela had become president
of the ANC Youth League. Under his leadership,
the ANC drafted a letter to Prime Minister
Malan. In it, they said that they had done
everything they could to legally gain rights for
blacks. They demanded a repeal of (end to) the
unfair apartheid laws. If no action were taken,
the ANC would have to use illegal means to
bring change.

Malan wrote back to the ANC. He said his
government would not meet their demands. He
said he would make sure whites ruled South

Africa. And he promised to use force to smash any black unrest. "We regarded Malan's [reply] as a declaration of war," Mandela wrote in his autobiography. The ANC got ready to take action. The group wanted to defy, or challenge, the government's laws. This was the start of the Defiance Campaign.

On June 26, 1952, ANC leaders called for a national strike. Blacks, East Indians, and coloureds marched through areas marked "Whites Only." They refused to carry their passbooks. (Nonwhite South African citizens were required to carry passbooks, which listed a person's race.) Malan did what he had promised. He called out the police, who arrested many strikers and treated them violently. Mandela, Sisulu, and others were arrested and later released.

The Defiance Campaign was mostly nonviolent. The protests were peaceful. The government arrested thousands of protesters. It also "banned" more than fifty strike leaders. Under South African law, a banned person was not allowed to travel or make public appearances. That person also could not speak with other banned people or do many other activities. By December

A police officer arrests a black woman for not carrying her passbook in the 1950s.

1952, arrests, bannings, and other government actions had halted the Defiance Campaign.

Yet the movement had gained ground. The ANC had created a united front against apartheid. It had focused world attention on the injustices in South Africa. ANC membership increased greatly.

Mandela and other leaders celebrated these successes. But at the same time, the government began a defiance campaign of its own. It banned most of the ANC leaders. It also declared that protesters could be whipped, jailed for up to three years, or fined nearly one thousand dollars. Or they could be

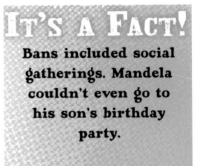

IT'S A FACT!
Bans included social gatherings. Mandela couldn't even go to his son's birthday party.

Crowds gathered in the streets to launch the Defiance Campaign of 1952.

These protesters took over a train compartment reserved for whites. They were arrested when they arrived in Cape Town.

given any two of these penalties combined. Anyone who encouraged protest could get an additional two years in prison or five hundred dollars in fines. These rulings forced the ANC to rethink its plans.

PRACTICING LAW

Meanwhile, Mandela managed to complete his law degree. In August 1952, Mandela asked his old schoolmate Oliver Tambo to join him in starting a law firm. Tambo was a brilliant law student and was committed to civil rights. The partners opened a law practice in downtown Johannesburg. Every morning, the two lawyers had to wade through long lines of waiting clients just to open their doors. Mandela later explained

Mandela and Oliver Tambo (left) worked together for many years.

why black South Africans needed so much help:

> Africans were desperate for legal help . . . it
> was a crime to walk through a Whites Only
> door, a crime to ride a Whites Only
> bus, . . . a crime to walk on a Whites Only
> beach, a crime not to have a pass book
> and a crime to have the wrong signature in
> that book, a crime to be unemployed and a
> crime to be employed in the wrong place,
> a crime to live in certain places and a
> crime to have no place to live.

The law partners turned out to be an excellent match. Tambo was the workhorse of the firm. Mandela was an excellent speaker. He was the perfect trial attorney. Together, they earned respect from the courts and other attorneys.

Meanwhile, the Mandela marriage was falling apart. Nelson loved his family. But his schedule often took him away from home. Even when he was in town, he worked long hours. He was becoming a stranger to his family.

By 1953, Nelson and Evelyn found themselves on entirely different paths. (They divorced in 1955.)

Mandela at his Johannesburg law firm

Nelson kept a strong relationship with his children. And he missed the life of a married man. But the civil rights movement called, and he continued to answer it.

UNITY ON TRIAL

The government continued to reshape South Africa to support apartheid. In 1953, the government passed the Bantu Education Act. With this law, church-run schools no longer received money to educate blacks. The law was clearly meant to keep blacks as ignorant as possible.

That year, some black communities responded by setting up their own schools. They were called "culture clubs." These schools were independent and couldn't be controlled by the government. But the government soon made these schools illegal.

Black leaders were outraged. They renewed their fight. Under the new leadership of Albert Luthuli, the ANC organized a People's Congress. The congress drew delegates (members) from all over the country and from all different ethnic groups. Even some whites were a part of the first meeting. They met in June 1955 in the small village of Kliptown, a few miles southwest of Johannesburg. More than three thousand people took part in the congress.

Dozens of passionate speeches created a sense of unity. But the real work of the two-day conference was writing the Freedom Charter.

The charter was hotly debated by delegates who feared its Communist tone. In the end, most were pleased with the document. But they never

Sign the FREEDOM CHARTER

THE PEOPLE SHALL GOVERN!	BATHO BA TLA BUSA!,	ZONKE IZINHLANGA ZIYOBA NAMALUNGELO ALINGANAYO!
ALL NATIONAL GROUPS SHALL HAVE EQUAL RIGHTS!	UKAROLO TSA SECHABA KAOFELA LI TLA BA TE TOIELA TSE LEKANANG!	BATE BAYODLA NGAKHEZO LUNYE!
THE PEOPLE SHALL SHARE IN THE COUNTRY'S WEALTH!	BATHO BA TLA KOFANELA LERUO LA LEFATSE!	IMNHLABATHI UYOCAZELWA LABO ABAWUSEBENZAYO!
THE LAND SHALL BE SHARED AMONG THOSE WHO WORK IT!	LEFATSE LE TLA AROHANYOA HAR'A BE LE LEMANG!	BONKE BAYOLINGANA PHAMBIKWOM- THETHO!
'ALL SHALL BE EQUAL BEFORE THE LAW!	BATHO KAOFELA BA TLA LEKANA IHLONIS LA MOLAO!	BONKE BAYOBA NAMALUNGELO ALINSANAYO!
ALL SHALL ENJOY EQUAL HUMAN RIGHTS!	BATHO KAOFELA BA TLA FUMANA LITOKELO TSE LEKANANG TSE TSOANETSENG BATHO!	KUYAKUBA KHONA UMSEBENZI NOKUNGASHUKUMISWA!
THERE SHALL BE WORK AND SECURITY!	MOSEBETSI O TLA ANELA HO BE LE TS'IRELETSO!	AMINTANGO YEMFUNDO NEMPUCUKO JIYOVULWA!
THE DOORS OF LEARNING AND OF CULTURE SHALL BE OPENED!	MENYAKO EA THUTO LE EA TSA BOTHO, E TLA BULOA!	KUYOBA KHONA IZINDLU! — NOKUNGATHIKAMEZWA NOKUTHO KOMALA!
THERE SHALL BE HOUSES, SECURITY AND COMFORT!	HO TLA BA MATLO, TS'IRELETSO, LE HO LULA MOTHO A PHOTHOLLOHILE!	KUYAKUBAKHONA UXOLO NOBUDLELWANE!
THERE SHALL BE PEACE AND FRIENDSHIP!	HO TLA BA KHOTSO LE SELEKANE!	

Among the authors of the Freedom Charter were Albert Luthuli *(upper left)* and Walter Sisulu *(third from lower left).*

got to vote on it. On the second day of the conference, police charged the speaker's platform. They pushed delegates off the stage and accused them of treason. The government said they were betraying their country.

Within three months, the South African government responded to the People's Congress. The police arrested anyone suspected of opposing government policies. In December 1956, Mandela was arrested. He, along with 155 others, was to be placed on trial for high treason.

The arrests were meant to silence those who disagreed with the government. But the arrests did just the opposite. Because of banning orders, many people had been unable to talk with one another outside of prison. Now they found themselves together in large cells. Old friends got

to know one another
again. Younger activists
listened and learned.
Instead of feeling despair,
prisoners felt an air of
celebration. They realized
they had a power that
the government could
not control.

Soon Mandela and
the other prisoners were
released. But they were

under strict banning orders until their trials. They
could not travel or speak in public.

REVOLUTIONARY LOVE

In the fall of 1957, Mandela put his time and
energy into the upcoming treason trials. If he and
the other men were found guilty, they faced long
prison terms. It would also be a big blow to the
movement. Those thoughts weighed heavily on
Mandela's mind as he moved through the traffic of
downtown Johannesburg one day.

He passed the finest black hospital in the city.
There, standing at the bus stop, was a beautiful

young woman. He could not help craning his neck to get a better look at her. Mandela was surprised by his interest in the woman. His marriage had fallen apart largely because of his involvement in the ANC. Without actually admitting it, he had accepted the lonely life of a civil rights activist. Still, the woman at the bus stop made him want to stop and talk. But there were other matters that required his attention. He had no time for romance. So he drove on by.

Over the next few weeks, he found himself thinking about the woman at the bus stop. He couldn't forget her face. Then he was amazed one day to see the woman seated in the office of his law partner, Oliver Tambo. She and her brother were there to discuss a legal problem.

Mandela listened to what they had to say. But he had a hard time concentrating. About the only thing that stuck in his memory was her name, Nomzamo Winifred ("Winnie") Madikizela. It meant "going through trials, one who strives." He knew the signs of love, and he didn't fight the feeling. Instead, he asked Winnie on a date.

On their first date, Nelson talked about his political life and the treason case. He also told her that he wanted to marry her. The couple began to see each other regularly. She met his two children and watched him work out at the gym. She went with him on many activities. He saw that Winnie was as committed to freeing black South Africans as he was. Within a year, on June 15, 1958, the couple married in the Transkei region.

Winnie's parents were proud to have such a famous and respected man in their family. Still,

Mandela and Winnie Madikizela were married on June 15, 1958.

Winnie's father warned her that she was not just marrying a man. She was marrying the ANC as well. He also warned that she might be criticized for marrying a divorced man. Traditional African society frowned on divorce.

From the beginning, Winnie and Nelson's lives were dominated by politics. Even to get married, forty-year-old Nelson had to apply to get his banning order lifted for a short period. Only then could he travel. He was allowed to leave Johannesburg to travel to Transkei for his wedding.

IT'S A FACT!

Soon after they married, Mandela tried to teach Winnie how to drive. Most black South African women didn't have this skill. During the lesson, both lost their tempers. Mandela stormed out of the car and walked home. Winnie simply taught herself. It was more than an hour before she drove herself home.

ON TRIAL FOR TREASON

The Mandelas did not have much of a honeymoon. The treason trial opened the same month they were married. Charges had been dropped against most of

the original protesters. But charges stood against
thirty of the most important figures, including
Mandela. He sat in jail while the trial went on.

During the high-profile trial, unrest continued
in the black townships. A peaceful protest took
place at a train station in 1960. A group of blacks
refused to present their passbooks to police. Police
opened fire. They killed 69 people and wounded
another 180. The incident was called the
Sharpeville massacre. The world condemned
the massacre.

The 1960 Sharpeville massacre caught the world's attention.

The black community in South Africa responded with more protests. The government declared a state of emergency. This allowed authorities to take away from blacks even more rights and to arrest even more people. Again, the crackdown had just the opposite effect of what was intended. With more of its leaders in jail, the ANC had a chance to plan new actions.

In the treason trial, government lawyers tried to prove that the ANC was a Communist organization. The lawyers said the ANC wanted a Communist government in South Africa. The trial lasted several years and cost a small fortune in legal expenses. But in the end, on March 29, 1961, Mandela and the other men were found not guilty.

As Mandela and the others left the courthouse, they were greeted by enthusiastic crowds. People cheered and sang. Mandela was pleased that he was free. But he knew that the authorities were going to work harder next time to make sure that the activists stayed in jail.

CHAPTER 6

IN HIDING

IN 1961, the banning orders against Mandela ran out. He had his public voice back. But he went underground (in hiding) to preserve it. The police were frantic to keep an eye on him, but Mandela hid.

For the first time in years, he traveled to the countryside. His banning orders had kept him in Johannesburg for nearly ten years. He had almost forgotten the natural beauty of rural South Africa. He met with rural activists and with journalists. He explained his positions and argued his points. He wrote letters to students. Students were becoming a powerful force in the struggle against apartheid.

SEARCHING FOR MANDELA

The police ran a huge manhunt looking for Mandela, but they didn't find him. By this time, he and Winnie had two daughters, Zenani and Zindziswa. He visited them whenever possible. He usually slipped in and out late at night. He had a few close calls, but he managed to stay one step ahead of the police.

His courage and daring were legendary in the black townships. Mandela sparked hope in young South African blacks. At the same time, he angered the South African government.

During this period, Mandela and a few ANC members formed a radical group called Spear of the Nation. The ANC had largely been nonviolent. But time after time, peaceful protest had been met with police violence. It had ended in further losses of the rights of black South Africans. Spear of the Nation decided to try another way.

The group set up headquarters at a farm in a suburb of Johannesburg. They decided to do

In Hiding

Mandela became famous when he went into hiding. Many Africans delighted in the reports they heard about his narrow escapes from authorities. He used several disguises. He grew out his hair. He changed the way he walked. Instead of commanding everyone's attention by striding into a room, he walked without confidence. He often posed as a gardener and wore blue overalls. When he drove a car, he posed as a white man's driver. He used false names.

damage to property and to the economy. These actions would put pressure on the government to make changes. But the leaders were careful to plan acts that would not harm people. They worked out their plans during September, October, and November of 1961. Mandela lived at the farm during this period. He was also able to spend some happy moments with his wife and children.

At the same time, the world was recognizing nearly fifty years of ANC nonviolent protest. In early December 1961, former ANC president Albert Luthuli became the first African to be awarded the Nobel Peace Prize. Within a week, on December 16, Spear of the Nation

In 1961, Albert Luthuli *(left)* became the first African to win the Nobel Peace Prize.

bombed sites in Johannesburg, Port Elizabeth, and Durban.

The explosions rocked white South Africa to its core. Finally, white South Africans began to listen to the problems of black South Africans. At the same time, the South African government began to prepare for a war between the races.

IT'S A FACT!

December 16 is an Afrikaner holiday that celebrated an Afrikaner victory over a Zulu leader in 1838.

That same month, the ANC was invited to the Pan African Freedom Movement conference in Ethiopia. The conference would unite leaders from all over Africa. The ANC decided to send Nelson Mandela as its representative. But he was not sure that he should go.

Mandela had promised he would not leave the country in this time of danger. If African blood were to be spilled, he said, his would mingle with the rest. But Albert Luthuli and the others finally convinced Mandela to go. In January 1962, he sadly said good-bye to Winnie and his children. Then he slipped out of the country.

Mandela went to the Pan African conference. He also toured East Africa, West Africa, and North Africa. He visited the heads of African nations that had only recently freed themselves from colonial rule. He exchanged ideas with people who would lead their countries in the years to come. He received military training in Algeria. That country had won independence from France barely two years earlier. Other African leaders believed in Mandela's cause. Some gave money. Others committed themselves to training ANC members.

In 1962, Mandela *(left)* was out of the country illegally. He met with leaders of the Algerian army during his tour of North Africa.

Mandela then traveled to Britain. There he found politicians willing to discuss the situation in South Africa. He created quite a stir whenever he traveled, and the media took notice. His opponents in Pretoria, the capital of South Africa, watched and waited.

After seven months of travel, Mandela returned to the country of his birth. He was happy to see his family and friends again, but he was also sad. South Africa had not changed in his absence.

ARRESTED AGAIN

Back home, he again took up his life on the run. By now, he had become a hero to blacks, East Indians, coloureds, and even whites who believed in real democracy. To the South African government, he was the most dangerous man in the country.

Mandela had become a legend. He had traveled and made connections all over the world. He could have easily remained in comfortable exile (life outside of one's homeland). The authorities would probably have welcomed that. They might even have allowed his family to join him out of the country.

IT'S A FACT!

A Xhosa favorite food is sour milk. Mandela was very fond of it. While in hiding, he often left a container of milk on a windowsill so it would curdle and grow sour.

Yet Mandela was a different sort of leader. He would make whatever sacrifice was necessary to win equal rights for all in South Africa. After nearly seventeen months on the run, Mandela was arrested in August 1962. He was put in a prison called the Johannesburg Fort. He was charged with encouraging people to strike and with leaving the country illegally.

South Africa's laws became even harsher during this time. The Sabotage Act, for example, increased penalties for trespassing, illegal possession of weapons, and other crimes. Banning of individuals became even more severe. Under the new laws, a banned person could not publish writings, receive visitors, or broadcast statements. Banned people had to report regularly to the police.

Meanwhile, criticism of apartheid grew in the rest of the world. The world had begun to condemn South Africa. Its government felt like it was under attack. It became defensive and prepared to do battle.

UN SANCTIONS

In late 1962, the United Nations (an organization that works for world peace and security) voted in favor of sanctions, or penalties, against South Africa. The sanctions were meant to punish South Africa for its human rights abuses. The countries that took part in the sanctions refused to do business with South Africa. For example, UN members could not sell weapons, aircraft, and other military equipment to South Africa. UN countries closed factories and business offices. They hoped to hurt South Africa economically as a way to force the government to make changes.

To the government, Mandela was a new national threat. The government planned to deal with him harshly.

At the court hearing following his arrest, Mandela saw many familiar faces in the courtroom. He knew the judge and some of the lawyers from his years of practicing law. He also noticed that they seemed uneasy, even ashamed. He was labeled the most dangerous man in South Africa—the worst outlaw possible. But the lawyers treated him with respect. He was Nelson Mandela, attorney at law, as far as they were concerned. Mandela realized that these people saw him as an ordinary man being punished for his beliefs. And they knew his beliefs were honorable.

That understanding helped Mandela shake off his depression at losing his freedom. He knew that the world saw him as a symbol of justice in the court of an unfair government. This feeling grew in the weeks leading up to the actual trial.

ON TRIAL

On October 15, 1962, Mandela's trial began in Pretoria. Mandela ran his own defense. The government felt they finally had him where they wanted him. They thought they would silence him, humble him, and break him.

But the old freedom fighter had something else in mind. Had the authorities forgotten that he was a lawyer who loved trials? He was exactly where he needed to be. Crowds of supporters and journalists gathered from around the world. Everyone sensed that something big was about to take place.

As the trial opened, Mandela strode proudly into the packed Pretoria courtroom. He wore a traditional

Mandela found power in wearing traditional Xhosa clothing during his trial in 1962.

Xhosa kaross, or cape. He looked like a Xhosa king walking into a royal kraal to be crowned.

"Power," someone shouted and thrust a clenched fist into the air. "The power is ours," another voice called. Then nearly everyone in the gallery (courtroom audience) rose and chanted "Power" until the pounding of the judge's gavel silenced them. Winnie was there too. She was also

Winnie Mandela also arrived at her husband's trial in Xhosa dress.

wearing Xhosa dress. This brought a smile to her husband's face.

Nelson Mandela wanted the world to know that this was not the trial of one man. He was not alone. Mandela planned to put the country itself on trial. Mandela asked for and was granted more time to put together his case. He returned to court on October 22, 1962.

The prosecutor (lawyer who opposes the defendant), Bob Bosch, respected Mandela for his legal work. Still, he did his best in the case. He called more than one hundred witnesses. Mandela questioned the witnesses forcefully. He pressed them hard. The atmosphere in the courtroom was tense. All the same, the prosecution had strong evidence against Mandela. It appeared he had indeed left the country illegally and had encouraged workers to strike.

It was then the defense's turn to present its case. Mandela surprised everyone. He announced that he would call no witnesses. He also announced he was resting his case (he was finished defending himself). The judge, prosecutor, and spectators were shocked. Whispers rippled through the gallery. The prosecutor fumbled for words. He had not expected

Crowds gathered outside the courthouse to show their support for Mandela.

to have to make his closing argument so quickly. Finally, he simply asked the court to find the defendant guilty on both counts (charges). The court went into a short recess (break).

THE SENTENCE

Then the court session began again. The judge summed up the charges and asked if Mandela had any closing remarks. He certainly did. He spoke for nearly an hour. He never denied that he had traveled outside the country without the government's permission. He never denied encouraging blacks to stay home from work. But he said that he wasn't a criminal. "I have done my duty to my people and to South Africa," he said. "I have no doubt that [people in the future will say] that I was innocent and that the criminals that should have been brought before this court are the members of the government."

After another short recess, the judge returned. In November 1962, he gave Mandela a sentence of five years in prison. Mandela's sentence was harsh. Some people in the courtroom responded with wails and weeping. Without knowing for sure, Mandela felt Winnie must have been among them. The punishment would hurt her almost as much as him. Still, Mandela stood tall and proud. He raised a clenched fist to the gallery. The crowd roared.

The crowd's response showed Mandela that his personal sacrifices were worth it. He was filled with love for the African people and for all those who were struggling to end apartheid. But what moved him to tears was the singing of the South African national anthem.

Winnie and her husband had only a few minutes to say good-bye. Despite the pain she was feeling, she wore a brave face. She did not cry. She never forgot that she was also a partner in the struggle for equality.

PRETORIA CENTRAL PRISON

Mandela was taken away in a police van. He heard the crowd of supporters singing in his honor. He held the face of Winnie in his mind, and his spirits soared. However, soon other faces came to mind: his young children, Zenani and Zindziswa, as well as his sons Thembelike and Makgatho from his first marriage. His longing for them was enough to make him weep.

Mandela went first to Pretoria Central Prison. Within a short time, he was transferred to Robben Island. The Island, as it was often called, was all too familiar to the Xhosa. The windswept rock was four miles off the coast of Cape Town. It had been a prison ever since the Dutch had settled in Africa in the 1600s. Many Xhosa had served prison time there.

The Island held white prisoners, but black prisoners faced the worst treatment there. People like Mandela, who were convicted of political crimes, received the very worst treatment. Mandela's clothes were taken. He received a pair of baggy shorts, a prison shirt, and sandals. He and the other African prisoners were not allowed to wear long pants like white prisoners, even in winter when the temperature often dipped below freezing. The prison dressed the black prisoners like children to remind them that it thought of them as children.

Mandela was transferred back to the prison in Pretoria a few months later. He soon learned that other members of the ANC had been arrested. They faced charges of sabotage for the Spear of the Nation bombings. Sabotage is destroying a company's property in order to interfere with the work taking place there. The government charged Mandela with sabotage too.

"I Am the First Accused"

In April 1964, Mandela and the other ANC prisoners were taken to South Africa's Supreme Court for the sabotage trial. There, he spoke publicly for the first time in more than a year. "I am the first accused," he said. It was the beginning of a long statement that introduced the defense's case in the trial.

Mandela explained that Spear of the Nation felt it had no other choice than violence. "All lawful modes of expressing opposition to this principle [apartheid] had been closed by legislation [laws], and we were placed in a position in which we had either to accept a permanent state of inferiority, or defy the government," he said.

Mandela's voice filled the courtroom. Most of white South Africa had never thought about these things. He explained that the ANC leaders had agonized over what to do when nonviolence failed. He said the ANC had no choice but to give in or to fight back. Spear of the Nation had chosen to commit sabotage–but only sabotage that would cause no loss of life.

Mandela was eventually found guilty of four counts of sabotage. He was sentenced to life in prison along with several other ANC leaders, including Walter Sisulu.

BEHIND BARS

The South African government set out to break Mandela's spirit and to stamp out his memory. The

WINNIE'S ROLE

After Nelson was sentenced to prison, Winnie spoke out for him in public. She continued his fight for human rights. The South African government watched her every move. The police harassed her. Government officials made it difficult for her to visit her husband. While she lived in Johannesburg, she was repeatedly banned and imprisoned. None of these problems prevented her from fighting for the movement.

government hoped people would forget about him. But he was not so easily forgotten. Many people grieved his imprisonment. And his wife was left to explain things to the children and to hold the family together.

Year after year, Mandela survived the hard prison life. Through most of it, Walter Sisulu was there with him. In prison, Mandela kept up a routine of physical exercise. He ran in place and did sit-ups and push-ups. He kept his mind sharp through study and, when possible, discussion. Even within the prison walls, news from the outside seeped in. Mandela kept up with it.

In prison, blacks and whites were treated differently. White prisoners wore long pants while blacks had to wear shorts. Whites got better medical care and better food. Prisoners and international leaders protested and, over time, conditions improved. Eventually, black prisoners won some rights. They were allowed to talk to one another. They received better food, long pants, and more blankets.

Mandela and his fellow ANC prisoners came up with sneaky ways to communicate with one another. They hid messages in the food containers that came from and were returned to the kitchen. They wrote messages in milk, which is almost invisible until someone sprays it with a common cleaning spray. One of the most popular ways to communicate in secret on Robben Island was writing small, coded messages

IT'S A FACT!

While in prison, Mandela was allowed to make a garden in the prison courtyard. He grew all types of vegetables. He shared the food with the guards as well as the inmates. Another hobby was playing checkers. At Christmas, the prisoners competed in fierce checkers tournaments. Mandela often faced off with a prisoner named Don Davis. Their games became one of Mandela's favorite ways to pass the time in prison.

on toilet paper. The guards discovered the messages and began to limit toilet paper. Prisoners soon received only eight squares of toilet paper a day.

Prisoners on Robben Island were expected to do work throughout the entire day, resting only for lunch and dinner. This work included crushing stones in the courtyard or gathering limestone in a rock quarry (mine). The prisoners often became stiff and sore from the labor. Mandela helped organize the efforts to improve living and working conditions at the prison. In this way, his stay on Robben Island was just another phase in the fight against injustice.

Prisoners worked splitting rocks in the Robben Island prison yard.

THE RUMOR MILL

Mandela had a hard time finding ways to communicate with his supporters. As a result, rumors about him spread far and wide. An injury to his heel made it necessary for Mandela to be hospitalized briefly. Reporters said he was on his deathbed. He complained to Winnie about the dampness in the prison. This became a story about entire cell blocks being flooded. A message about his shoes being too tight turned into the news that one of his toes was being cut off. There was little Mandela could do to stop the rumors.

FIGHTING INJUSTICE FROM PRISON

During these years, Mandela's name became a rallying cry. By the mid-1970s, black students were leading the struggle for democracy in South Africa. The South African government treated protesters like enemies of the state. Police cracked down brutally.

Things came to a tragic head in 1976. Afrikaans, the language of the Afrikaners, became a required course in South African schools. Students did not want to be forced to learn the language of the rulers. So students at all levels refused to go to school. The largest of these school boycotts took place in Soweto Township.

The protests began peacefully. But the
government allowed no defiance. The police moved
in on the township. Over sixteen months, about
one thousand people died and about four thousand
were injured in clashes between police and
protesters. Most of those killed and injured were
children. Thousands of students were jailed. Some
spent up to five years in jail, while others were
never heard from again.

Thirteen-year-old
Hector Peterson
(being carried) was
the first person to die
in the 1976 Soweto
uprising.

The best-known student activist was Steven
Biko. He was beaten to death in police custody in
1977. A young East Indian named Ahmed Timol
was killed in a fall from the tenth floor of police
headquarters in Johannesburg. Other student
leaders also died mysteriously. Those who survived
were banned.

Around the world, people were joining the
movement. They went to rallies that demanded the
release of South Africa's political prisoners. In 1980
Oliver Tambo and the ANC created the "Release
Mandela" campaign. Free Mandela posters and
graffiti were everywhere. In 1985, students at U.S.

Antiapartheid protesters gather in New York City in 1985.

colleges joined in a nationwide protest. Rallies were held in major cities, including Atlanta, New York City, and Washington, D.C. The hard work of protesters, diplomats, and the public pressured the South African government to rethink its position.

The United Nations continued to condemn apartheid. Many countries increased the sanctions against South African companies and South African products. South Africa's economy was in very bad shape. Eventually, the South African government realized that something had to be done. It decided to work with Mandela to bring change to South Africa.

7

FREE AT LAST

SOUTH AFRICAN LEADERS had seen that
Mandela was just as powerful in prison as out.
Over the years, they had tried to release
Mandela from prison—but only if he would do
what they asked. They wanted Mandela and
the ANC to give up violence and illegal
protests. But each time, Mandela said no.
Each time, he had chosen to stay in prison
rather than cooperate with apartheid. In July
1989, South African leaders arranged for
Mandela to meet with South Africa's
president, P. W. Botha.

President Botha was known to have a fierce temper. He was nicknamed the Great Crocodile. So Mandela was surprised that the meeting turned out to be friendly. The two men discussed South African history, although from very different points of view. Then Mandela began to talk about the problems in modern South Africa. He said there could be no real negotiations between white and black leaders until political prisoners were released.

Not surprisingly, Botha said that he could not do this. The meeting ended. Still, Mandela felt good about it. He saw that all the political pressure and social unrest were leading to change.

MANDELA AND DE KLERK

A month later, however, Botha resigned from office. F. W. de Klerk became president. No one thought he'd be any more sympathetic to black freedom than others in the government had been. Still, negotiations between Mandela and the government continued.

Mandela held firm to his demands. He again requested that all political prisoners be released. In exchange for a democratic and racially free South

Africa, Mandela promised that black leaders would not cause trouble.

Mandela watched the new president and sized him up. He became hopeful by what he saw. When there was a demonstration, de Klerk did not ban the leaders, as other presidents had. He did not respond with police brutality. Instead, he simply instructed the leaders to make the demonstration peaceful. That, in itself, was a change.

Finally, in October of 1989, de Klerk did something Mandela had waited nearly thirty years to see. He released a number of political prisoners. Among them was Mandela's longtime friend and mentor, Walter Sisulu. Then, on December 12, de Klerk and Mandela held a meeting.

The two men did not see eye to eye. But Mandela later described de Klerk as a thoughtful man who was willing to listen and think matters

IT'S A FACT!

Soon after his release from prison, Sisulu became the ANC's deputy president. He retired in 1994, just before South Africa's first multiethnic elections. He died in 2003.

through. A major disagreement between Mandela and de Klerk was the president's idea of "group rights." De Klerk wanted to preserve power for white South Africans, regardless of election outcomes. Mandela would not accept this idea. It looked to him like the government was not really willing to end apartheid.

De Klerk thought more about it. On February 2, 1990, he showed that he was sincere. Standing before Parliament, he announced sweeping changes. The changes would take down apartheid. He announced that the government would lift the bans on the ANC, the Communist Party, and thirty-one other antiapartheid organizations. The government would also free political prisoners, end segregation in public places, and lift other restrictions.

MANDELA FREED!

A few days later, on February 11, 1990, Nelson Mandela was freed from prison. He'd spent twenty-seven years in prison. In the great square in front of city hall in Cape Town, a crowd of people greeted him. Great applause filled the air as Mandela stepped to the

Mandela and his wife, Winnie, raise their fists in celebration as Nelson leaves prison after twenty-seven years.

microphone, his wife Winnie at his side. He raised his fist in victory.

"Friends, comrades, and fellow South Africans," he started in a clear voice. "I greet you all in the name of peace, democracy and freedom for all. I stand before you not as a prophet but as a humble servant of you, the people."

Shortly after his release from prison, Mandela met with the ANC leaders. They were pleased to see him free, but he had been in prison for a long time. Was he the same leader? Mandela put the leaders' fears to rest. By the end of the meeting, he was elected deputy president of the ANC.

Mandela then traveled to meet with leaders throughout Africa, Europe, and the United States. He was amazed at the enthusiasm he met wherever he went. The leaders were impressed with his strong beliefs, his great mind, and his lack of bitterness. Mandela did not focus on revenge. Instead, he focused on what was best for the future of his country.

FAMILY STRUGGLES

His public life was a series of successes. But his family life was difficult. As Nelson worked to bring all South Africans together, Winnie's politics had become more radical. She had changed because of her many years of police harassment. She'd formed a group called the Mandela United Football Club. The club members terrorized black Africans. She and the club were accused of kidnapping and other crimes. Winnie denied any involvement in the crimes, but she became less involved with the club. Over time, her political views fit less with the overall ANC goals. The couple had also drifted apart in personal ways.

In April 1992, Mandela announced that he and Winnie had separated. (They divorced in 1996.) He was careful to explain that he still loved and respected her. He regretted the pain his family had experienced. The sacrifices he and his family had made were great. But he felt they had to be made if a new nation were to come into being.

Throughout his personal troubles, Mandela continued his political work. He negotiated with the government to create a new political system. Negotiations were not always easy. Radical forces on both sides tried to disrupt the process. However, on June 3, 1993, Mandela presented a formula for a new political system. It gave rights to all South Africans no matter what their race. A national vote would be held the following year. It would not be restricted by race. Each person would get one vote.

It was a historic turning point. Mandela and President de Klerk were both rewarded for their efforts later in 1993. Together, they accepted the Nobel Peace Prize in Oslo, Norway. Mandela applauded de Klerk's

IT'S A FACT!

Mandela's friend Oliver Tambo died in 1993. This was a year before South Africa held its first multiethnic presidential election. His life and death were honored with a ceremony.

Mandela and de Klerk receive the 1993 Nobel Peace Prize.

efforts. Together, they had moved the nation
beyond the dark past of racial hatred.

PRESIDENT MANDELA

The end of apartheid brought the first election in
which all South Africans could vote. Black South
Africans finally had a say in running their country.

The man they wanted for president was Nelson Mandela. On May 2, 1994, Mandela won the presidential election and became the first black president of South Africa. He made it his duty to heal the wounds of the past.

"This is one of the most important moments in the life of our country," he said during his victory speech. "I stand here before you filled with deep pride and joy—pride in the ordinary...people of this country.... This is a time to heal the old wounds and build a new South Africa."

A week later, Nelson Mandela was sworn into office. He looked out upon a sea of faces. In the audience were leaders from around the world, journalists, and comrades in the struggle. They saw Mandela, a man of dignity and strength, take the oath of office and address the crowd with these words:

> Out of the experience of...human
> disaster that lasted too long, must be born
> a society of which all humanity will be
> proud.... We have, at last, achieved our
> political [freedom].... Never, never, and
> never again shall it be that this beautiful

land will again experience the oppression of one by another. . . . The sun shall never set on so glorious a human achievement. Let freedom reign. God bless Africa!

In 1996, Mandela oversaw the creation of a new South African constitution. That year, Mandela set up the Truth and Reconciliation Commission. This panel investigated accounts of political crimes committed under apartheid. He appointed noted South African civil rights leader Bishop Desmond Tutu to head the commission. The commission began its work in 1996 and issued its final report in 1998. The aim of the report was to identify individuals who had committed crimes during apartheid and to find out the truth about what happened. "Only the truth can put the past to rest," Mandela said.

To encourage people to tell the truth, those who confessed to crimes committed during apartheid were not punished. Many black South Africans, including many members of the ANC, disagreed with the Truth and Reconciliation Commission and wanted stronger punishments for those responsible for apartheid.

STILL AT WORK

In 1998, on his eightieth birthday, Mandela married Graca Machel. She is the widow of the former president of Mozambique, a neighboring African nation. In 1999, Mandela retired from politics. He decided not to run again for president. Since that time, he has continued to work for peace all over the world.

In July of 2003, Mandela stated that he had not done enough to fight AIDS (acquired

Mandela addresses South Africa's Parliament in Cape Town on May 10, 2004.

immunodeficiency syndrome) while he was
president. He has devoted himself to fighting the
disease, which has killed
millions of Africans,
including one of his sons.
About 5.3 million of South
Africa's 45 million people
live with HIV (human
immunodeficiency virus)–
the virus that causes

IT'S A FACT!

In early 2005,
Mandela's oldest
living son, Makgatho,
died of AIDS.

AIDS. That is more than in any other country. His
great fame has encouraged many to join the
struggle with him. He will be remembered for his
fight against AIDS as well as for his historic efforts
to bring freedom to South Africa. He continues to
stand for justice throughout the world.

PRONUNCIATION GUIDE

Afrikaans	ah-free-KAHNS
apartheid	ah-PAHR-tayt
Botha	BWEH-thah
Gaur Radebe	GAU RAH-dee-beh
Graca	GRASHA
Jongintaba	jun-geen-TAH-bah
kaross	KEH-rohs
Luthuli	loo-TOO-lee
Madikizela	mah-dee-kee-ZAY-lah
Makgatho	ma-gha-THOO
Mbekela	mbeh-KEH-lah
Meligqili	meh-lee-KEE-lee
Mfengu	m-FENG-goo
Mkakaziwe	mkah-KAH-zee-way
Mphakanyiswa	m-pah-gah-NEEZ-wah
Mqhayi	mgah-EEE
Mvezo	m-YEH-zo
Nyathi Khongisa	n-yathi KON-geh-sah
Qunu	KOO-noo
Rolihlahla	ho-lee-SHAH-shah
Soweto	soh-WAY-toh
Thembu	TEM-boo
Transkei	trahn-SKY
Xhosa	KOH-sah
Zenani	ZEN-ahn-nee
Zindziswa	zin-ZEE-swa

Afrikaner: a white South African with Dutch roots

apartheid: a set of laws that gave the best jobs, education, voting rights, medical care, and other rights to whites

bachelor's degree: a certificate awarded to a person after he or she has finished four years of study at a college or university

banning: under apartheid, a law that stopped a person from publicly opposing the government by speaking or writing

coloured: the name the South African government once gave to a nonwhite South African who had Asian roots

Defiance Campaign: a 1952 plan in which large groups of nonwhites publicly defied, or challenged, apartheid laws

East Indian: a person whose roots are in India. (This term is used to avoid confusion with "Indian" as a reference to a Native American.)

ethnic group: a group of people who share the same language and culture

Freedom Charter: a 1953 document that said all South Africans should have equal rights and be able to share the country's wealth

Mandela United Football Club: a youth group set up in Soweto in the late 1980s by Winnie Mandela

passbook: a government-issued notebook once carried by every nonwhite in South Africa. It listed a person's race.

political prisoner: a person who has been put in jail because of his or her political opinions

racial discrimination: unjust behavior toward others based on a person's race

regent: a person who makes decisions for a king or queen who is too young to rule

sabotage: damaging or destroying property on purpose

sanction: a penalty or punishment

Spear of the Nation: founded by Nelson Mandela, a group that practiced sabotage to end apartheid

township: under apartheid, an area set aside for black residents

Truth and Reconciliation Commission: a panel of South Africans that was set up after apartheid ended. The commission's job was to hear and publicize information about abuses under apartheid.

white supremacy: the idea that white people are better than all other people

SOURCE NOTES

5 "Statement of the President of the African National Congress Nelson Rolihlahla Mandela at his Inauguration as President of the Democratic Republic of South Africa Union Buildings," *ANC.org*, May 10, 1994, http://www.anc.org.za/ancdocs/history/mandela/1994/inaugpta.html (June 9, 2005).

5 Ibid.

6 Ibid.

24 Nelson Mandela, *Long Walk to Freedom: The Autobiography of Nelson Mandela*, (Boston: Little, Brown, 1986), 26.

27 Ibid., 36.

41 Ibid., 64.

51–52 Ibid., 95.

53 Ibid., 110.

58 Ibid., 130.

81 Ibid., 332.

83 "I Am Prepared to Die: Nelson Mandela's Statement from the Dock at the Opening of the Defense Case in the Rivonia Trial," *ANC.org*, April 20, 1964, http://www.anc.org.za/ancdocs/history/mandela/1960s/rivonia.html (June 9, 2005).

84 Ibid.

96 "Nelson Mandela's Address to Rally in Cape Town on his Release from Prison," *ANC.org*, February 11, 1990, http://www.anc.org.za/ancdocs/history/mandela/1990/release.html (June 9, 2005).

100 Mandela, 619.

100–101 "Statement of the President of the African National Congress Nelson Rolihlahla Mandela at His Inauguration as President of the Democratic Republic of South Africa Union Buildings," *ANC.org*, May 10, 1994, http://www.anc.org.za/ancdocs/history/mandela/1994/inaugpta.html (June 9, 2005).

101 Lynne Duke, "South Africa Establishes Truth Panel," *WashingtonPost.com*, July 20, 1995, http://www.washingtonpost.com/wp-srv/inatl/longterm/s_africa/stories/truth072095.htm (June 9, 2005).

SELECTED BIBLIOGRAPHY

Benson, Mary. *Nelson Mandela: The Man and the Movement.* New York: W. W. Norton, 1986.

Denenberg, Barry. *Nelson Mandela: "No Easy Walk to Freedom."* New York: Scholastic, 1991.

Hughs, Libby. *Nelson Mandela Speaks: Forging a Democratic, Nonracial South Africa.* New York: Pathfinder, 1993.

Mandela, Nelson. *Long Walk to Freedom: The Autobiography of Nelson Mandela.* Boston: Little, Brown, 1986.

Mandela, Nelson. *Struggle Is My Life.* New York: Pathfinder, 1986.

Mutwa, C. Vusamazulu. *Africa Is My Witness.* Cambridge, MA: Blue Crane, 1966.

Nelson Mandela's Speeches. March 10, 1998. Available online at http://www.anc.org.za/people/mandela/ (June 2005).

FURTHER READING AND WEBSITES

African National Congress
http://www.anc.org.za
The official website of the ANC includes photos, biographies, and writings about the ANC and its leaders, as well as the organization's history.

Beecroft, Simon. *The Release of Nelson Mandela.* Milwaukee: World Almanac Library, 2004.

Connolly, Sean. *Nelson Mandela.* Chicago: Heinemann Library, 2001.

Denenberg, Barry. *Nelson Mandela: "No Easy Walk to Freedom": A Biography.* New York: Scholastic, 1991.

Downing, David. *Apartheid in South Africa.* Chicago: Heinemann Library, 2004.

Grant, Karima. *Nelson Mandela*. New York: Children's Press, 2005.

Green, Robert. *Nelson Mandela: Activist for Equality.* Chanhassen, MN: Child's World, 2003.

Hargrove, Jim. *Nelson Mandela: South Africa's Silent Voice of Protest*. Chicago: Children's Press, 1989.

Hughes, Libby. *Nelson Mandela: Voice of Freedom*. New York: Dillon Press, 1992.

Katz, Bobbi. *Meet Nelson Mandela*. New York: Random House, 1995.

Kramer, Ann. *Nelson Mandela*. Austin, TX: Raintree Steck-Vaughn Publishers, 2003.

Meltzer, Milton. *Winnie Mandela: The Soul of South Africa.* New York: Puffin Books, 1987.

Nelson Mandela Foundation
http://www.nelsonmandela.org/
The Nelson Mandela Foundation website includes information about the foundation, as well as speeches, press releases, and pledge information.

Nelson Mandela Web Page
http://www.anc.org.za/people/mandela/
Part of the ANC website, this Web page contains links to documents and articles written by and about Nelson Mandela. The page also includes photos and a biography page that includes an extended and brief biography.

Van Wyk, Chris. *Oliver Tambo*. Cape Town: Maskew Miller Longman, 1994.

PHOTO ACKNOWLEDGMENTS

The images in this book are used with permission of:
© Louise Gubb/CORBIS SABA, p. 4; © National Archives of
South Africa, #TAB 36025, p. 11; © UWC RIM Mayibuye
Archives, pp. 14, 22, 28, 30, 32, 42, 44, 47, 54, 55, 61, 64, 66, 73,
77, 80, 87; © Roger De La Harpe; Gallo Images/CORBIS,
p. 19; © The McGregor Museum/The Duggan-Cronin Collection,
p. 20; © Bettmann/CORBIS, pp. 38, 50, 56, 57, 90; © Bailey's
African History Archives, p. 39; © Jurgen Schadeberg, p. 59;
© Time Life Pictures/Getty Images, p. 71; © AP/ Wide World
Photos, p. 78; American Lutheran Church used by permission of
Augsburg Fortress, p. 89; © Allan Tannenbaum/ZUMA Press,
p. 96; © Reuters/CORBIS, p. 99; © MIKE HUTCHINGS/
Reuters/Corbis, p. 102. The map on page 8 is by Laura Westlund.

Cover image: © David Turnley/CORBIS.